100 Questions and Answers About Hmong Americans

Secret No More

Michigan State University School of Journalism

Front Edge Publishing

For more information and further discussion, visit:

biasbusterguides.com

Cover design by Rick Nease

RickNeaseArt.com

Published by

Front Edge Publishing

42807 Ford Road, #234

Canton, Michigan, 48187

Front Edge Publishing books are available for discount bulk purchases for events, corporate use and small groups. Special editions, including books with corporate logos, personalized covers and customized interiors are available for purchase. For more information, contact Front Edge Publishing at info@FrontEdgePublishing.com

Contents

These are the authors of "100 Questions and Answers About Hmong Americans." From left, first row: Wendy Guzman, Demonte Thomas, Taylor Truszkowski, Claire Grant. Second row: Jeanne Stuart, Kelly Branigan, Erin Tremonti, Caroline Turner, Alexandra Simmons. Third row: Kate Townley, Brandon Carey, Ethan Gallagher, Rin Haddon, Kamal Lea, Donovan Scott. Also, Ava Okros and Charlie Bernet. Bias Busters veteran Lacie Kunselman of The TJX Companies, Inc., in Massachusetts, helped with the editing.

Acknowledgments

The community editor for this Bias Busters project is **Julie Xiong**. She helped us plan this project months in advance, visited the class and was one of our readers. You will also find her work in the introduction and in a couple of video vignettes.

Joseph Yang grew up on the south side of Lansing, Michigan. He obtained his bachelor's degree from Michigan State University and his law degree from Thomas M. Cooley Law School, where he graduated cum laude. He serves the community as a lawyer and with Hmong organizations. With Julie Xiong, he was on stage for our community Q&A about Hmong people and traditions.

Tyler Lee is a communications manager in the Department of Physiology at Michigan State University, where he earned his degree in journalism. Lee helped break the ice early in the semester by teaching the students to play pov pob and came back later with some wonderful traditional Hmong clothing and jewelry.

A tenured professor at Michigan State University, **Dr. Geri Alumit Zeldes** is both an academic and a practitioner. She has a dozen best paper awards from international communication associations and more than 100 screenings and awards for her documentary work.

Haitau Yang encouraged this project months in advance and advised its launch. He has held top executive board positions with Michigan State's Hmong American Student Association and its Asian Pacific American Student Organization. Yang majored in applied engineering sciences with a concentration in supply chain management.

The **MSU Hmong Students Association,** the **Hmong Family Association of Lansing, Michigan,** and the **Hmong American Community of Lansing** welcomed us at events, including picnics and mixers.

The following people helped edit the questions and the answers or made other contributions. Their knowledge and work helped ensure this guide's accuracy and authority.

Dr. Melissa Borja is author of "Follow the New Way: American Refugee Resettlement Policy and Hmong Religious Change." She is a core faculty member in the University of Michigan's Asian/Pacific Islander American Studies Program. She is a senior adviser to the Religion and Resettlement Project led by Princeton University's Office of Religious Life, and she advises the U.S. Conference of Catholic Bishops

April Cha is an artist and senior instructional designer at the University of California, San Diego. She has a bachelor of arts degree in English Language and Literature from the University of California, Riverside.

Txongpao Lee, executive director of the Hmong Cultural Center in St. Paul, Minnesota, explained clan origins in Southeast Asia.

Nancy Yang is senior editor for audience engagement at the Star Tribune in Minneapolis. Before that, she worked for Minnesota Public Radio, Internet Broadcasting and the

Pioneer Press in Saint Paul, Minnesota. She has served on the National Advisory Board to the Asian American Journalists Association.

Nancy Ngo has spent more than 25 years as an award-winning journalist in the Twin Cities, first with the St. Paul Pioneer Press and then the Star Tribune. She has served as a national officer with the Asian American Journalists Association.

Nzong Xiong is an outreach and communications representative with the San Joaquin Valley Air Pollution Control District. She was a reporter with the Lexington Herald-Leader and then the Fresno Bee for more than 10 years. Xiong earned a bachelor's degree in journalism at the University of Missouri-Columbia and was an intern with the St. Paul Pioneer Press and The New York Times.

Frances Kai-Hwa Wang is a journalist, teacher, speaker, activist and poet. She focuses on diversity, race, culture and the arts. Her work has appeared at NBC News Asian America, at PBS NewsHour, PRI Global Nation, New America Media, Pacific Citizen, Angry Asian Man, Cha Asian Literary Journal, Kartika Review, Drunken Boat, and several anthologies, journals and art exhibitions.

Mai Kou Vang, owner of Ming Dynasty Chinese Cuisine in East Lansing, Michigan, prepared a tasty Hmong meal for the class. Her daughter, **Maizoua Hang**, explained the meal to the students.

Michigan State University has two published authorities on Hmong cultural arts. They are **Dr. C. Kurt Dewhurst** and **Dr. Marsha MacDowell**. Dewhurst is director for arts and cultural partnerships and a senior fellow in University Outreach and Engagement. MacDowell is director of the Michigan Traditional Arts Program in the Residential College in the Arts and Humanities. She is also a professor in the Department of Art, Art History, and Design. At the MSU Museum, Dewhurst is curator of Folklife and Cultural Heritage; MacDowell is curator of Folk Arts and Quilt Studies. **Lynne Swanson**, cultural collections manager, opened the museum's trove of Hmong artifacts to us.

Thanks to **Brant Wells**, senior director of television and digital operations at WKAR at Michigan State University and his crew for taping our community conversation about Hmong Americans. **Aidan Binford**, an MSU student in journalism and music performance, produced the four video vignettes in this guide from that conversation.

Michigan State students under the guidance of Design-Artist-in-Residence **Richard Epps** made the graphics.

We appreciate the support of **Dr. Tim P. Vos**, professor and director of the Michigan State University School of Journalism.

"100 Questions and Answers About Hmong Americans: Secret No More" is made possible in part by a grant from Michigan Humanities, an affiliate of the National Endowment for the Humanities. Michigan State University and the School of Journalism are very grateful for this association and support.

Introduction

By Julie Xiong

Hmong Americans are Americans of Hmong ethnic ancestry. Hmong people began arriving in the United States in the 1970s after being provided with political asylum, refugee status and citizenship because of their unique contributions to the United States. Hmong combat soldiers served under the direction of the United States military and clandestine forces from 1961-1975, in the Secret War of Laos, during the Vietnam War. All Hmong American families share a common history, rooted in painful memories associated with this war and powerful stories around the hope, pursuit and desire for a better future here in America.

As a first-generation-born Hmong American, my siblings and I grew up listening to these stories. My father was the first in his family to cross the Mekong River, known to some as the river of tears. He found a boat that secretly took Hmong people over to Thailand to escape persecution. He waited with fear to board the boat and when he finally did, he looked back and saw that the group he was with had been tracked down and escorted away. To his relief and great sadness, he made it to the other side. Unfortunately, this was not the case for many, including some of his siblings and my grandparents, who died trying to cross the river of tears.

At first, these stories felt like secrets shared and understood only among the elders who had experienced the war first-hand. With each story, I found myself yearning to learn more. Asking questions and listening without passing judgment has introduced me to the most interesting and fulfilling conversations. Although most Americans know nothing about the contributions of the Hmong being recruited by the CIA to support covert operations overseas, the more than 300,000 Hmong living in the United States are evidence that this war existed. I encourage everyone, including the next generation of Hmong Americans, to learn about this history and keep the conversations going.

This brief guide introduces the readers to this community through a journalistic lens. It is important to understand that lived experiences of previous generations have played a key role in shaping the different perspectives and practices of Hmong Americans today. We understand that there may be varying views of the 100 answers provided in this guide. Thus, we welcome and encourage the discussions to continue, as understanding will not come from one guide or a set of 100 questions, but through dialogue that fosters understanding over time.

Julie Xiong has worked with Asian American and Hmong organizations nationally, across Michigan and in local communities. She is a community and social impact leader, making meaningful change in the community for more than 20 years. Xiong earned bachelor's and master's degrees from Kettering University and studied in George Washington University's Executive Leadership Development Program.

She has been a board member of the Leadership Education for Asian Pacifics nonprofit based in Los Angeles and advisory board chair for the Council of Asian Pacific Americans. She has been engaged with the Michigan Asian Pacific American Affairs Commission and continues to be an active contributor to nonprofits like the Asia Society and OCA-Asian Pacific American Advocates.

Foreword

By Gia Vang

We descended into Laos, a country I had never stepped foot in, a country that belonged to my mother and father first. Tears welled up as I peered out of the plane window to see lush, green jungle, the jagged edges of the mountains, the red dirt that created webs of roads and walking paths in and around villages and towns. I had only heard stories about this land for 37 years, the landscape only existing in my mind.

In 1975, my parents, Choua Thao and Tsong Tong Vang, fled Laos amid conflict and violence and made a harrowing journey to a Thai refugee camp. They, along with my eldest sister, arrived in the U.S. on May 9, 1980, part of a wave of Hmong refugees trying to escape the loss and heartbreak of the Secret War and holding onto dreams of what was to come.

I was born in California.

As new Americans, my family, along with many other Hmong families, were now tasked with how to survive and thrive in this new land while simultaneously holding onto the distinctive customs and traditions that made us Hmong. The children born in the U.S., like me, would have to navigate building bridges between the old and new ways of being.

Today, Hmong people in America are confronting real challenges to our culture, one that prides itself on a sense of collectiveness.

One is language loss. Those around my age often share similar stories of serving as our parents' translators at governmental or medical offices, making sure mail was read and translated, and speaking as representatives of our parents during phone calls. We learned English well enough, but it came at a cost. Some of us felt forced to grow up quickly, and Hmong, as a primary language, began experiencing a decline in use in the United States.

Additionally, there is debate within the Hmong American community about ideas around religious beliefs, family structures and expectations, interracial dating, patriarchy, political beliefs, and the place of traditional customs, among other issues. As a group and as individuals, we must decide what no longer serves us and what to keep and hold dearly.

Yet, the idea of thriving has been ever present in our roughly 50 years in America. We have our first Olympic gold medalist of Hmong descent in Sunisa Lee. Sheng Thao is the first Hmong person to be mayor of a major U.S. city in Oakland, California. Several Hmong chefs have been nominated for the coveted James Beard Awards over the past few years. Our culture has produced a handful of actors in Hollywood, some of whom have played a role in major films. I am the first Hmong news anchor in a major news market. All of these people come from refugee families. As we explore the next evolution of our culture in the U.S., we hold true to the notion that we are a proud indigenous people whose history began long before they lived in Southeast Asia.

The plane finally touched down on the tarmac in Vientiane. I wiped away my tears and grabbed my suitcase. The plane door opened to stairs for the passengers. As I took my first step, I was struck with the humid air and the deep realization that the beauty of being Hmong in America is only one piece of being a Hmong person in the world.

Gia Vang is an Emmy-award winning television news anchor and reporter. Her journalism work has taken her all over the country, including stops in Oregon, Missouri, Arizona, Minnesota and parts of California. Vang is the daughter of Hmong refugees from Laos. She grew up with eight siblings in Sacramento and has a journalism degree from Sacramento State. Vang is also the co-founder of the Very Asian Foundation, a nonprofit that seeks to shed light on Asian experiences through advocacy and celebration. The movement was sparked after a fellow journalist shared a racist voicemail on social media.

Preface

Hmong Americans have traveled a long way in a very short time.

Very few Hmong people lived in the United States until its 1975 pullout from Vietnam. That put Hmong people, recruited by the U.S. Central Intelligence Agency to fight a secret war against the Viet Cong, in grave danger. Thousands were killed; thousands were evacuated to the United States to build new lives. They came from Southeast Asia and were scattered among states including California, Minnesota, Wisconsin, Michigan and North Carolina.

Most Hmong people arrived with only what they could carry. They had little formal education, savings, warm clothing or any connection to these new places. Their English was limited. Families had been split up. Belief systems were disrupted. Return was impossible because the nomadic Hmong people did not even have a homeland. As Joseph Yang, one of the people you will meet in this guide, said, his people have had to "carry our culture and our religion on our backs."

In fewer than 50 years, Hmong Americans have traveled further still. Today, this population has very high rates of U.S. citizenship. They are succeeding in college, business, government and the arts.

They have been elected or appointed to local, state and federal offices. They are judges, doctors, college students and professors. Many work in agriculture, as their families did in Southeast Asia before they were recruited to fight. Others work in U.S. health, education and media.

Hmong artists have enriched the tapestry of their new country with traditional music, song, poetry and visual arts. Some are excelling at U.S. forms of writing, dance and music. That includes hip-hop, which emerged in the 1970s, around the time so many arrived.

Despite their success, Hmong Americans are still something of a secret. The United States has not come as far in accepting and understanding them as they have come in adjusting. Hate crimes, ignorance and anti-Asian bias are still problems.

Answers to questions about origins, identity, beliefs and resettlement are here to help people have better conversations with their Hmong neighbors.

The Michigan State University School of Journalism thanks the Hmong community for its work on this guide. We hope you read the guide and then take the next step by getting to know some of these still-new Americans. They may be your neighbors, co-workers, classmates, and acquaintances.

This guide was suggested by Nancy Ngo, a reporter in Minnesota, where there is a large Hmong community, in hopes of uniting people.

Joe Grimm
Series Editor
Bias Busters
Michigan State University School of Journalism

Identity

1 Are Hmong people a race, nationality, ethnicity or culture?

They are an ethnic group with a shared history and culture. Because they never had a country of their own, they do not have a nationality.

2 Is there a Hmong homeland?

Having migrated frequently, often fleeing from armed enemies, Hmong people lived in other people's countries. They could not simply declare their own. Consequently, they do not have a homeland to which they can return.

3 Where did Hmong people originate?

Hmong people are believed to have originated about 5,000 years ago in north-central Asia as a nomadic people. Over hundreds of years, they migrated south into Tibet and then China. For thousands of years, Hmong people lived independently while making tribute payments to the Chinese government.

4 Why did they leave China?

In the 1800s, during China's last dynasty, Hmong people were oppressed. Their written language was outlawed, and political oppression followed. The Hmong people rebelled. Confronted by persecution, declining soil fertility and a growing population to feed, some migrated to Southeast Asia. They settled in the mountains of what are now Laos, Thailand, Vietnam and Myanmar.

5 Are Hmong people Chinese?

They are neither ethnically nor culturally Chinese. They have a distinct language, traditions and beliefs that differ from those of the Chinese. In the years since they settled in Southeast Asia, they have grown even more distinct. While the Hmong and Chinese share some cultural and historical connections, they have their own identities and traditions.

6 Are Hmong people Mongolian?

People often ask this. Despite similar sounding names, Hmong and Mongolian people are not the same. Both cultures have different origins and histories. Hmong people migrated into and through China to Southeast Asia, while Mongolian people are native to Mongolia in Central Asia. Hmong people speak a language from the Hmong-Mien language family, while Mongolian comes from the Mongolic family.

Language

7 What is the Hmong language?

The Hmong language has two main dialects: Green, also called Blue Hmong or Mong Leng, and another called White Hmong. These dialects evolved because of separation in China. While the words are the same language, pronunciation can be very different. Among Hmong Americans, White Hmong is dominant.

8 Are Miao and Hmong the same?

Miao covers ethnic groups located primarily in southern China's mountains and includes Hmong people. Most Miao groups are not Hmong. Some Hmong people find it insulting to be called Miao. Clues are in an article, "What Is the Actual Number of the (H)mong in the World?" by French anthropologist Jacques Lemoine. He wrote that, before 1949, "Miao was a kind of vague category, something like 'aborigine' which was used to classify all strange and backward-looking non-Han people in southern China."

9 How do we say Hmong?

The "H" is essentially silent, and the "O" is long, like the vowel in "home." Here is the pronunciation as Nancy Yang voiced it for Minnesota Public Radio: soundcloud.com/user-13159522/how-to-say-hmong

10 What does Hmoob mean?

Hmoob and Hmong mean the same thing and are pronounced the same way. "Hmoob" is the way "Hmong" is spelled in the Hmong language. Hmong is transliterated as Hmoob in White dialect and as Moob in Green dialect. Capitalized as HMoob, it acknowledges both dialects.

11 How is Hmong spoken?

Hmong has short words, often just three letters or parts each. The first part gives the consonant sound, the second is a vowel and the third marks the tone used for that word. Hmong also has puffs, or aspirations from the nose, before or after some words. The aspirated "H" in "Hmong" is what makes the word sound like it begins with "M."

12 Is Hmong difficult to learn?

Language difficulty depends on how similar a new language is to the one the learner already knows. For most English speakers, tonal languages such as Hmong can be hard to learn. In tonal languages, the rise or fall in tone has meaning. According to the "Field Guide to Hmong Culture," there are seven or eight tones. Descriptions

English proficiency of U.S. Hmong population

Percentage of people 5 and older who are English proficient

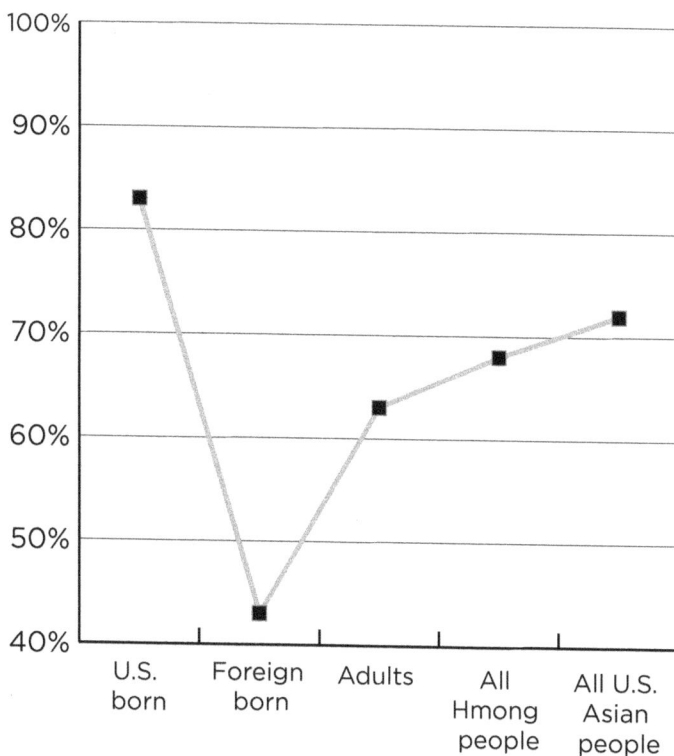

Source: Pew Research Center analysis of American Community Survey data, 2019

Graphic by Zachary Urbin

include "high tone," "high falling tone," "low tone," "low falling tone," and "breathy mid-low tone." Two words with the same sounds can mean something entirely different depending on the tone.

13 Is there a written language?

In the 1600s, China's Qing Dynasty outlawed Hmong writing, records and histories. Spoken Hmong survived. Stories, folklore and culture couldn't be written down but survived through embroidery. In the 1950s, efforts began to revive written Hmong. The Roman Popular Alphabet was made to record Hmong words. In 1959, a semi-syllabic alphabet called Pahawh Hmong was created. Although Hmong is still primarily a spoken language, some count as many as 16 writing systems for it today.

14 Is Hmong language similar to Chinese, Laotian and Thai?

Hmong language is distinct from those languages although there are shared roots. The Hmong, Chinese, Laotian and Thai languages are all tonal. Of the four, Hmong has the most tones.

U.S. Hmong population

Hmong population in the U.S.

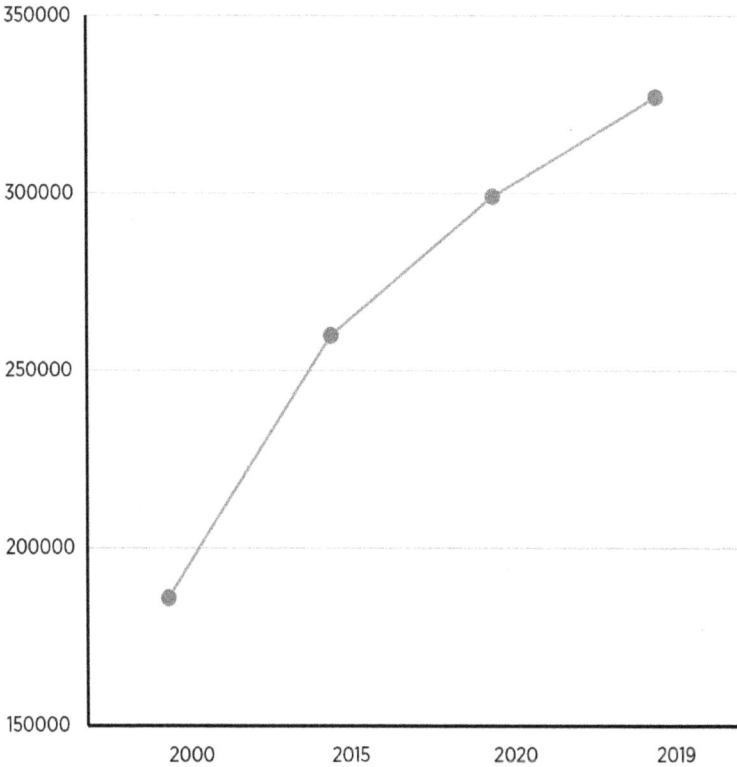

Source: Pew Research Center analysis of American Community Survey data, 2019

Graphic by: JaTasia Powers

Demographics

15 How many Hmong people live in the United States?

According to the U.S. Census Bureau's 2021 American Community Survey, there were 368,609 Hmong people in the country. About 230,000 were born in the United States. The population was 186,000 in 2000. About 95 percent of Hmong Americans are Hmong alone, according to the Census Bureau.

16 Where are the major U.S. population centers?

States with the largest Hmong populations are:

California 86,989

Minnesota 63,619

Wisconsin 47,127

North Carolina 10,433

Michigan 5,924

The top five U.S. cities are: Minneapolis-St. Paul, Minnesota; Fresno, California; Sacramento, California; Milwaukee-Racine, Wisconsin; and Hickory, North Carolina.

Top 10 U.S. metropolitan areas by Hmong population

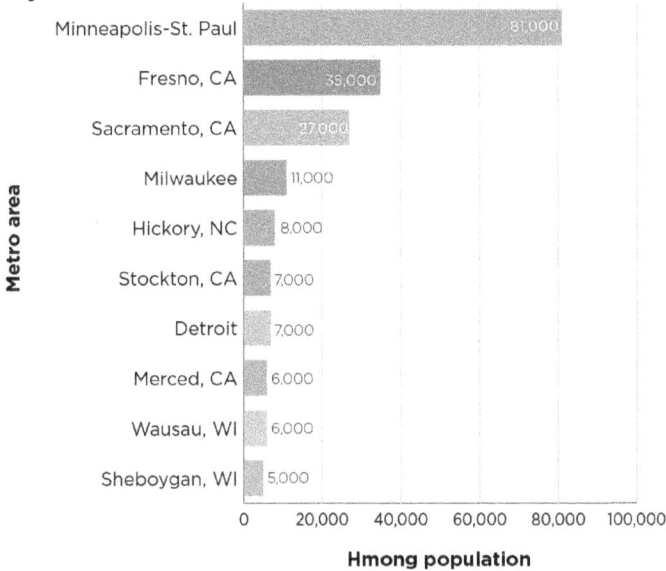

Metro area	Hmong population
Minneapolis-St. Paul	81,000
Fresno, CA	35,000
Sacramento, CA	27,000
Milwaukee	11,000
Hickory, NC	8,000
Stockton, CA	7,000
Detroit	7,000
Merced, CA	6,000
Wausau, WI	6,000
Sheboygan, WI	5,000

Source: Pew Research Center analysis of American Community Survey data, 2019
Graphic by Lina Saleh

17 How many Hmong people remain in Asia?

It is difficult to determine the number of Hmong people in Southeast Asia given the number of countries and various ways they conduct censuses. It is estimated 1.2 million Hmong people live in northern Vietnam, Laos, Thailand and eastern Myanmar.

The Secret War

18 What was the Secret War?

This was a secret military campaign waged by the
U.S. Central Intelligence Agency to stop the spread of
communism. In 1959, civil war broke out between the
Royal Lao government and the communist Pathet Lao.
Fourteen countries, including the United States, signed
the Declaration of the Neutrality of Laos. It called for
all foreign troops to leave Laos during the war. Another
signer of the neutrality agreement was the Soviet Union,
which backed the communists. France, which had begun
colonizing Southeast Asia in 1887, signed, too. France
had consolidated Laos, North and South Vietnam and
Cambodia and called them French Indochina. Laos
gained independence in 1960 after the French lost in the
Indochina war. However, France's continued ambitions
in the region contributed to the Vietnam War, which
had begun in 1955. Starting in 1961, the CIA secretly
recruited, trained and funded a surrogate army of Hmong
soldiers. The United States saw Laos as the place to stop
communism's southward spread. Hmong fighters were
pitted against the Vietnamese communists, or Viet Cong.

19 Why did Hmong people fight for the CIA?

Hmong people also opposed communism. They were hired to disrupt supply lines from Vietnam to Laos, spy, guard a U.S. radar station that directed bombing, and rescue downed American pilots.

20 What promises were made in exchange for help?

The CIA promised to protect and provide aid and to grant the Hmong people a pathway to the United States after the war. It did not promise help with resettlement or veterans' benefits.

21 Who led the Hmong soldiers?

The CIA recruited General Vang Pao. He had fought against Japan during World War II and the French in the 1950s.

22 When did the U.S. acknowledge the Secret War?

The first indication was a 1971 Congressional hearing that revealed the United States was dropping white phosphorus and cluster bombs on Laos. The U.S. was also deploying Agent Orange, designed to defoliate jungles. The effects of its exposure on humans include cancer, birth defects and life-threatening illnesses. From 1964 to 1973, Laos became the most heavily bombed country in history. Many of the bombs lay on the ground unexploded. Later in 1971, U.S. Sen. Ted Kennedy held hearings in Boston about the bombings. The hearings attracted little attention. Forty-five years later, in 2016, Barack Obama became the first U.S. president to publicly acknowledge the U.S. role in Laos. When he did, he announced a doubling of U.S. funding to remove unexploded bombs to $90 million over three years.

23 Who won the secret war?

The CIA and its Hmong fighters lost. The Royal Lao government fell. The United States quickly withdrew. Hmong people were declared enemies of Laos' new communist government and lost air support, supplies and food drops.

Displaced and Resettled

24 When did Hmong people come to the United States?

Hmong people came to the United States in waves. A few came earlier, but the first wave included about 3,500 people in the second half of 1975. These were mostly evacuated military personnel and their families. Another 44,000 Hmong people escaped to refugee camps in nearby Thailand by the end of 1975, according to the Migration Policy Institute. They later left the camps. About 15 percent of Hmong immigrants to the United States came in 1976-1979. Forty-six percent came in the 1980s, and 39 percent came in the 1990s. In 2003, a large unofficial refugee camp for Hmong people who had fled Laos closed. It was at a Buddhist monastery called Wat Tham Krabok in Thailand. This sent thousands of Hmong refugees to the United States from 2004 to 2006. Most followed relatives in California, Minnesota and Wisconsin.

25 How did Hmong people get out of Laos?

The first to flee were in an emergency military evacuation that began in May 1975. Thousands were evacuated from Laos and Thailand in unmarked U.S. military aircraft and taken to the United States. Thousands more escaped across the Mekong River, the third longest river in Asia. It has been estimated that between 1975 and 1985, 100,000 Hmong people died trying to flee Laos. Half that number drowned or were killed trying to cross the Mekong River between Laos and Thailand. Survivors waited in refugee camps in Thailand. Many Hmong children were born in the camps.

26 How did the United States classify Hmong people?

The Hmong were classified as political refugees. Since they had to leave their country due to the war, they could be admitted to the United States. However, the process could take years. Many lacked documentation, and family members needed to help them enter the United States.

27 Where else did the Hmong diaspora go?

France was one of the first countries to accept Hmong refugees, with many settling in the Alsace region. The Hmong diaspora also went to Australia, French Guiana, Canada, Germany and several other countries. According to the Migration Policy Institute, more than 200,000

Julie Xiong explains how Hmong people escaped from Laos. Follow the link: youtu.be/d2bKIquNlNU or scan the QR code to view.

Hmong people have fled Laos as refugees. About 90 percent settled in the United States.

28 Where did they settle in the United States?

Hmong people were dispersed. If there was a national plan for the refugees, it seems to have been to resettle them in different places. This would mean fewer worries for U.S. residents in any one area concerned about the sudden influx and potential competition for resources and jobs. Dispersion could speed assimilation and absorption. To keep federal expenses lower, settlement was left to churches and social service agencies. Wisconsin, California and Minnesota accepted the most.

29 Do Hmong soldiers receive veterans' benefits?

Hmong soldiers are not classified as U.S. veterans and do not receive most veterans' benefits. In 2018, more than 40 years after the conflict, the United States granted some death benefits under the "Hmong Veterans' Service Recognition Act." Benefits included a headstone or marker, a casket or cremation and burial in a Veterans Administration national cemetery. Burial in Arlington National Cemetery was not allowed. To qualify, veterans must have lived until March 23, 2018, and have citizenship under the 2000 Hmong Veterans' Naturalization Act. In late 2023, Wisconsin's Congressional delegation proposed making Hmong veterans of the Vietnam War eligible for the Congressional Gold Medal. Yee Leng Xiong, executive director of the Hmong American Center in Wausau, Wisconsin, said elders are afraid "the United States would no longer respect the Hmong community" once its veterans die.

30 Did Hmong refugees become U.S. citizens?

Eventually, most did. The Hmong Veterans' Naturalization Act of 2000 gave veterans who fought in Laos and their spouses 18 months to apply for citizenship. The act waived the U.S. Citizenship and Immigration Services English language test requirement and gave special consideration on the U.S. civics test.

Hmong more likely than other Asians to be citizens

Foreign-born Hmong people in the United States are 20% more likely than all foreign-born Asians in the U.S. to have become citizens.

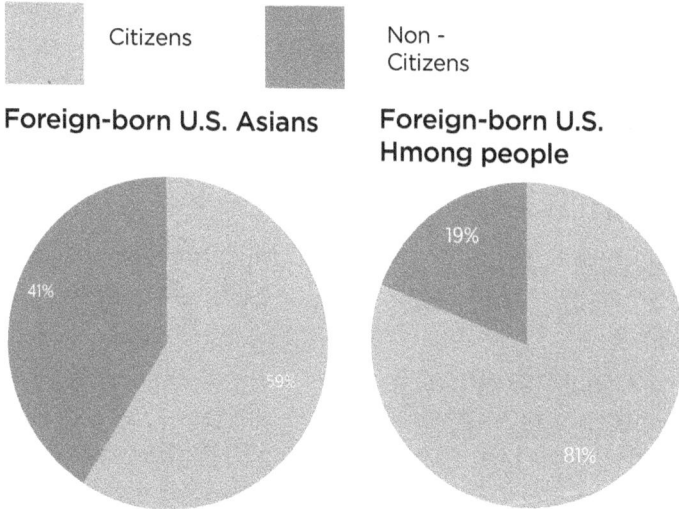

Citizens

Non - Citizens

Foreign-born U.S. Asians

Foreign-born U.S. Hmong people

41%

59%

19%

81%

Source: Pew Research Center analysis of American Community Survey data, 2019

Graphic by Trina Fiebig

31 Are more Hmong people coming to the United States?

The Hmong American Center in Wisconsin calls this unlikely. "The U.S. government has no plan to bring additional Hmong refugees to this country," the center reported. "The Thai government has repatriated most Hmong refugees in Thailand back to Laos," the center reported. National Public Radio reported that the Hmong community mobilized in 2020 against a plan by the Trump Administration to deport Hmong people to Laos. About

4,500 out of the 300,000 Hmong people in the United States, 1.5 percent, have deportation orders. This is usually because of criminal convictions. Orders can be issued over minor crimes and they can break up families or send people to countries where they have no connections or job prospects. The orders can stay in effect for decades, even after sentences have been served.

32 How did the U.S. government help the transition?

Hmong people came with little savings, formal education or occupational training. They also needed to learn English. The Minnesota Attorney General's office noted, "The federal government has failed to provide adequate and continuing refugee assistance ... When Congress originally passed the Refugee Act of 1980, it agreed to reimburse states for the cash and medical assistance that they provided to refugees during the first 36 months of resettlement. However, the time period covered by these payments has steadily declined."

33 Who helped the refugees resettle?

It was mainly Christian organizations such as Catholic Charities and Lutheran Social Services. The Church of Jesus Christ of Latter-day Saints began missionary efforts in the late 1970s and organized its first Hmong-speaking branch. Refugee organizations also helped. These groups set up housing, food, employment and community resources. Of course, Hmong people lifted each other up, too, as they tried to acclimate to new surroundings while holding onto their traditional culture.

Length of time in the U.S. for Hmong people

Length of U.S. residency for foreign-born Hmong

More than 10 years   0 to 10 years

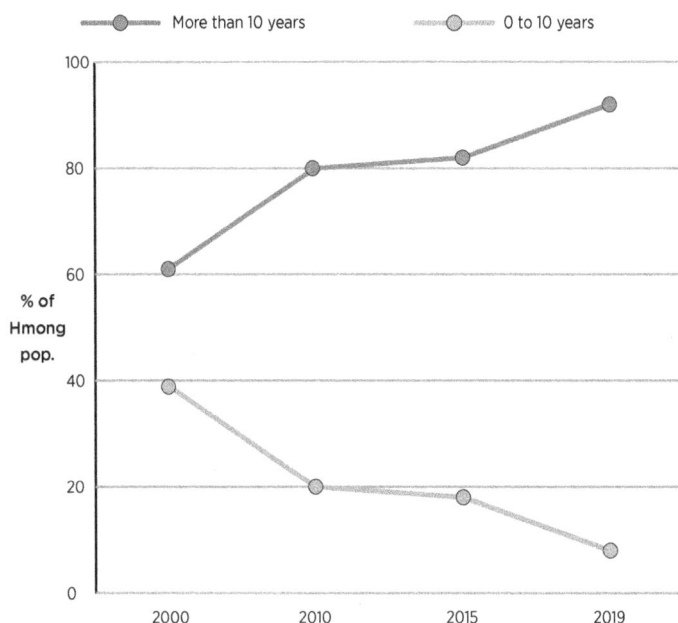

% of Hmong pop.

100
80
60
40
20
0

2000   2010   2015   2019

Source: Pew Research Center analysis of American Community Survey data, 2019

Graphic by Reese Anulewicz

34 How have Hmong people integrated into U.S. society?

This gets at how much people must change to be accepted. It is the difference between being accepted with one's values and traditions or being assimilated and vanishing. The Hmong American Center affirms that Hmong people are integrating. "A significant number of Hmong are graduating from high schools and colleges," the center stated. "Ninety-five percent of all able-bodied Hmong Americans are participating in the local workforce.

Nearly 70 percent of all Hmong families have become homeowners. In addition, a growing number of Hmong families are starting businesses such as grocery stores, restaurants, specialty stores, and small manufacturing companies."

35 What education did early Hmong immigrants have?

According to the 1988 report "The Hmong in America," by Donald A. Ranard, about three quarters of early Hmong refugees were illiterate with no educational background. Boys who did go to school might have gone only as far as third or fourth grade. Girls might have attended just first grade. Most Hmong refugees had little or no formal education in Laos or in Thailand's camps prior to coming to the United States. Reasons included a lack of schools and difficulty getting to them.

36 Are Hmong people catching up educationally?

Yes. By 2019, U.S.-born Hmong people over 25 were much more likely to have had some college than those born overseas. As a group, they were approaching the overall U.S. rates for college attendance.

Educational attainment for U.S. Hmong population

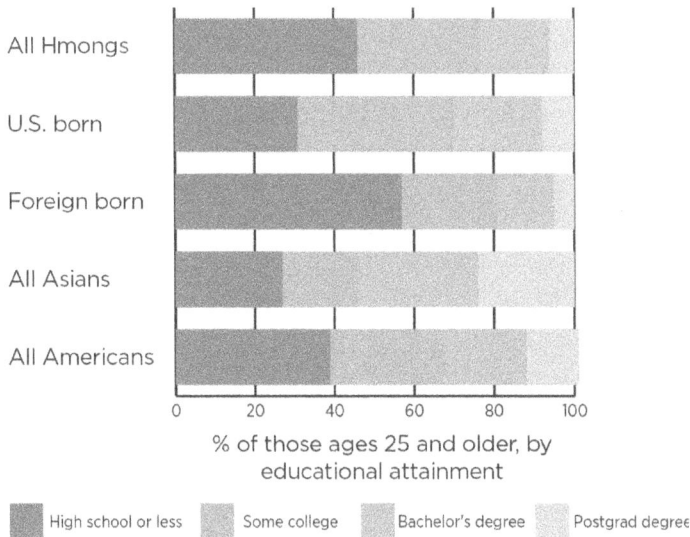

All Hmongs

U.S. born

Foreign born

All Asians

All Americans

0   20   40   60   80   100

% of those ages 25 and older, by educational attainment

■ High school or less   ■ Some college   ■ Bachelor's degree   ■ Postgrad degree

Source: Pew Research Center analysis of American Community Survey data, 2019

Graphic by Caroline Baratta

37 What is the model minority myth?

This myth is the stereotype that Asian American people are naturally successful, smart, hard-working or nice. It can be a wedge between ethnicities or nationalities. Also, the myth paints people within the group to be all alike, denying people individual credit for their success. Several studies have shown that the myth is false. Asian American people have a tremendous range of experiences, as is the case in all groups.

38 How does this myth affect Hmong people?

Among all Asian Americans, Hmong people are especially harmed by this myth. It compares people who arrived more recently with fewer resources and less education to those who have been in the United States for generations or who have more education and wealth. The myth can imply more recent arrivals appear to lack ambition.

Generations

39 What are the generations in the Hmong community?

This is complicated because generation and immigration definitions overlap. Context and definition are important. U.S. demographers parse people into 15- to 18-year generations. For example, in the general population, Generation Z was born from 1997 to 2012, and Millennials were born from 1981 to 1996. When speaking of immigration, however, people who arrived from another country can become first-generation Americans. Generation 1.5 Americans arrived in the United States as adolescents and grew up with two cultures. Second generation means people born in the United States to immigrant parents. For Hmong people, there is another generational perspective based on place, not age. Neng Thao was born in a Thailand refugee camp in 1993 and graduated from Harvard in 2015. He told the Twin Cities Monitor that people born in Laos, including his parents, are first generation. People born in refugee camps, like him, are second. The third generation are those born in the United States. People of the same age can belong to different geographic generations but the same one as someone who is 20 years older or younger.

Place of Birth

Hmong people are more likely than other Asians to have been born in the U.S.

U.S. Hmong place of birth

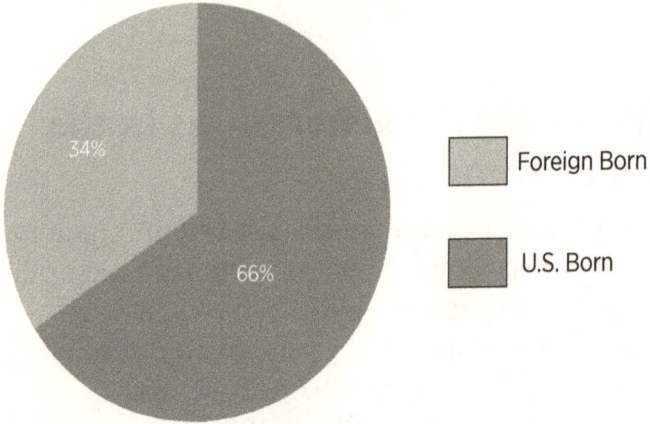

34%

66%

Foreign Born

U.S. Born

U.S. Asians place of birth

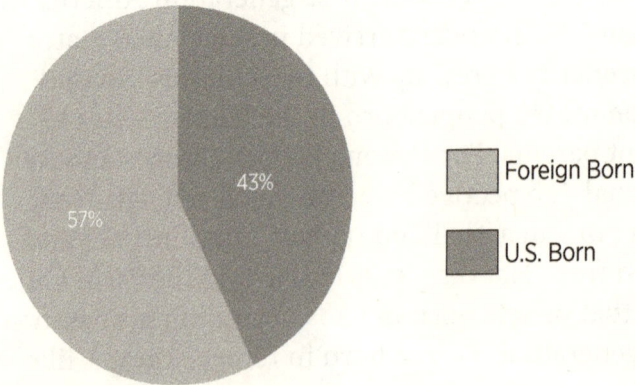

43%

57%

Foreign Born

U.S. Born

Source: Pew Research Center analysis of American Community Survey data, 2019

Graphic by Benjamin Edwards

40 Has this created generation gaps?

According to Thao, his parents were busy just trying to get by, and he did not want to bother them. As with many immigrant groups, language, culture and traditions are not always passed along easily. Thao wrote that growing up in the United States without their native culture can make Hmong people feel rootless. It can be difficult to maintain traditions while fitting in with other Americans their age. Children can feel cut off from elders and from non-Hmong people their own age. The presence and size of the surrounding Hmong community can affect this. Places where local communities embrace Hmong culture encourage greater participation.

Median Ages in the U.S.

Age groupings are by percentage. Compared to ages of U.S. Asians overall, this chart reflects the surge of immigration in the 1970s.

	All Asians in the U.S.	Among Hmong in the U.S.		
		All	U.S. Born	Foreign Born
Median age	34	25	18	41
Younger than 5	7	10	14	<0.5
5-17	17	24	35	4
18-29	18	27	32	15
30-39	17	19	16	25
40-49	14	9	1	24
50-64	16	8	1	24
65+	11	3	1	9

Source: Pew Research Center analysis of American Community Survey data, 2019

Graphic by Ahmarea Covington

This chart shows the effects of Hmong migration to the United States having been concentrated between 1975 and 2000. This comparison of Hmong people in the country to U.S. Asians overall shows higher proportions of foreign births in the 30-64 Hmong age bracket. Compared to other Asians in the U.S., very few Hmong Americans 17 and younger are foreign born.

Families

41 What is the role of the family in Hmong society?

Individual Hmong identities are tied up in their families. Clans, lineage and ancestors all spring from family. In the absence of nationality or homeland, family is the prime organizing connection. Family is central to spirituality, economics and belonging.

42 What size are Hmong families?

Hmong people came from mountainous regions where many children were needed to help with farming. This has been the case with agricultural communities all over the world. Since resettlement in the United States and reduced reliance on agriculture, families have become smaller. Today, a Hmong family in the United States with four or five children is not unusual.

43 What are gender roles?

Hmong American women are now rejecting traditional expectations that they are primarily wives and mothers who take care of the household. Traditional Hmong society is patrilineal, meaning household and clan membership is

Julie Xiong explains the Hmong family.
Follow the link: youtu.be/UmJrfrHJc6I
or scan the QR code to view.

passed from fathers to sons. When women marry, they join
their husband's clan and leave their own. Wives acquire
the social status of their husbands. Male children will stay
with the family and clan, but females who marry will leave.
According to tradition, two sets of family spirits cannot
live under the same roof, so a daughter who marries will
not worship her birth clan's spirits. Men are head of the
family and lead ancestor worship. Men hold more power
publicly, while women hold power privately. Women often
manage household finances and chores.

44 Has immigration changed roles?

There has been tremendous change. Women have many
more educational and employment opportunities today,
and two-income families are more necessary, according
to EthnoMed. Some young Hmong American women
report feeling pressure to "do it all." Professionally, they
feel they must have a good education and a job. Cultural

expectations for them as wives and mothers remain high. Many Hmong American women are still expected to listen to their parents' opinions about who they date. They often are encouraged to date Hmong American men, but the parents' hold is not as strong as it once was.

45 Are Hmong people LGBTQ-tolerant?

Some sexual identities and orientations have been taboo. Traditionally, gender-based roles have also discouraged some people from coming out. However, some members of the community have been pushing for recognition and organizing groups like Shades of Yellow. Keven Xiong, the organization's first executive director, told Twin Cities Daily Planet that the group was started in 2003 to create a safe space for Hmong members of the LGBTQ+ community to gather.

46 What is visiting etiquette in a Hmong home?

According to the Hmong Cultural Center in St. Paul, Minnesota:

- When meeting a family, first address the head of the household, typically the father.
- Show respect and humility.
- People are uncomfortable saying "no" directly, so they might say "yes," even if that is not what they mean.

- Smiles are good. However, too much eye contact can seem rude.
- Compliments about children might worry traditional families, who fear attracting attention from harmful spirits.
- Patting or touching a child's head can also alarm some parents.
- Unexpected visits are OK, but ask if it is a good time.
- Guests should accept offers of food and drink.
- Sit if invited, but do not linger at the table after a meal.

Dating and Marriage

47 What are traditional dating customs?

Couples might meet with a Hmong New Year's game. In pov pob, boys and girls line up facing each other. The girls begin by tossing a black cloth ball to a boy they like. As they pass the ball back and forth, they talk. They might also sing poetry, called kwv txhiaj. Anyone who drops the ball must give their partner an item they are wearing. Pov pob leads to meetings to retrieve items and could lead to courtship. The game is also played as an icebreaker.

48 At what age do Hmong people marry?

A tradition of marrying young has changed given today's economic realities and women choosing education and careers over tradition. In Laos, Hmong girls between the ages of 13 and 16 typically married older males. Most U.S. states have higher minimum ages for marriage. So, some couples will commit in the Hmong tradition but not marry until they reach the legal age.

49 Are marriages arranged?

This has become less common. The traditional custom was for both sets of parents to arrange an engagement. It was also OK for a couple to elope or engage without parental permission. Marrying someone who the parents don't approve of is discouraged.

50 What are some wedding traditions?

Typically, there are two paths to marriage. Traditionally, and more respectful to the bride's family, is for the groom to ask for her hand. More commonly, the bride follows the groom to his home. These choices affect one of the major wedding traditions, the dowry paid for the bride. The "bride price" symbolizes status, a new relationship between families, the bride's value to her family, and the promised security of marriage. The amount is discussed among male relatives of both families. This custom is still common in Hmong weddings. The dowry in the United States can range from $5,000 to $20,000 if the more traditional ways are followed. Customarily, it was paid in silver bars. The primary focus of a Hmong wedding is to unite the families. If dowry negotiation is long, ceremonies may last two days and one night. The wedding includes the bride and groom uniting, the bride being inducted into the family and the wedding at the bride's family home or a church. At the wedding, the groom must vow to the sky and to the Earth to love the bride and do what he has promised. Then the groom will pay his respects to the bride's mother and father and give them the dowry. The wedding concludes by gathering at the groom's home.

51 Are some wedding traditions declining?

One of the biggest taboos in Hmong marriages is to not marry within the same clan. Clan identity passes from father to child, so a person is allowed to marry into their mother's clan but not the father's. Yet, such marriages happen. "Bride kidnapping" is now rare even in countries Hmong people are from, and the tradition is not common in the United States. Another diminishing tradition is men taking a second wife. The expense of dowries made this a rich man's practice. Polygamy is not legal in the United States.

Marital status of U.S. Hmong people

	All Asians	Hmong in U.S.		
		All	U.S. born	Foreign born
Marital status (18 and older)				
Married	59	44	28	59
Divorced/Separated/Widowed	11	9	3	16
Never married	30	47	68	25

Source: Pew Research Center analysis of American Community Survey data, 2019

Graphic by Lily Cross

Colors, Clans and Kin

52 What are clans?

Clans are extended families. They are the main organizing system among Hmong people. Clans provide social and economic support and authority. The limited number of clans is why many Hmong people seem to have the same surname.

53 How many clans are there?

There once were 12, but today 18 are recognized. Some people even recognize 21. The 18 largest are Cha (Chang), Chue (Chu), Cheng, Fang, Hang, Her (Herr, Heu), Khang, Kong, Kue, Lor (Lo, Lao), Lee (Le, Ly), Moua (Mua), Pha, Thao (Thor), Vang (Va), Vue (Vu), Xiong and Yang (Ya).

54 What is Hmong lineage?

Lineage is the group of people who share the same clan name going back in history. With historical data, records and oral history, Hmong people can trace their families back many generations.

55 What do White, Green, Black, Blue and Striped Hmong mean?

Colors reflect traditional clothes worn by different groups. The Black Hmong are known by the traditional indigo blue that they wear. They are also known for their handicrafts. The White Hmong, for whom the main dialect is named, wear decorated white pleated skirts. Blue/Green Hmong wear decorative indigo batik textiles. Striped Hmong are recognized by their intricate jacket sleeves, which have three to four black or blue stripes. The Striped Hmong speak the White Hmong dialect. The map on the right shows the approximate areas of origin for different Hmong groups in Southeast Asia. Credit: Rendered by Ethan Gallagher with information from Txongpao Lee, executive director of the Hmong Cultural Center in St. Paul, Minnesota.

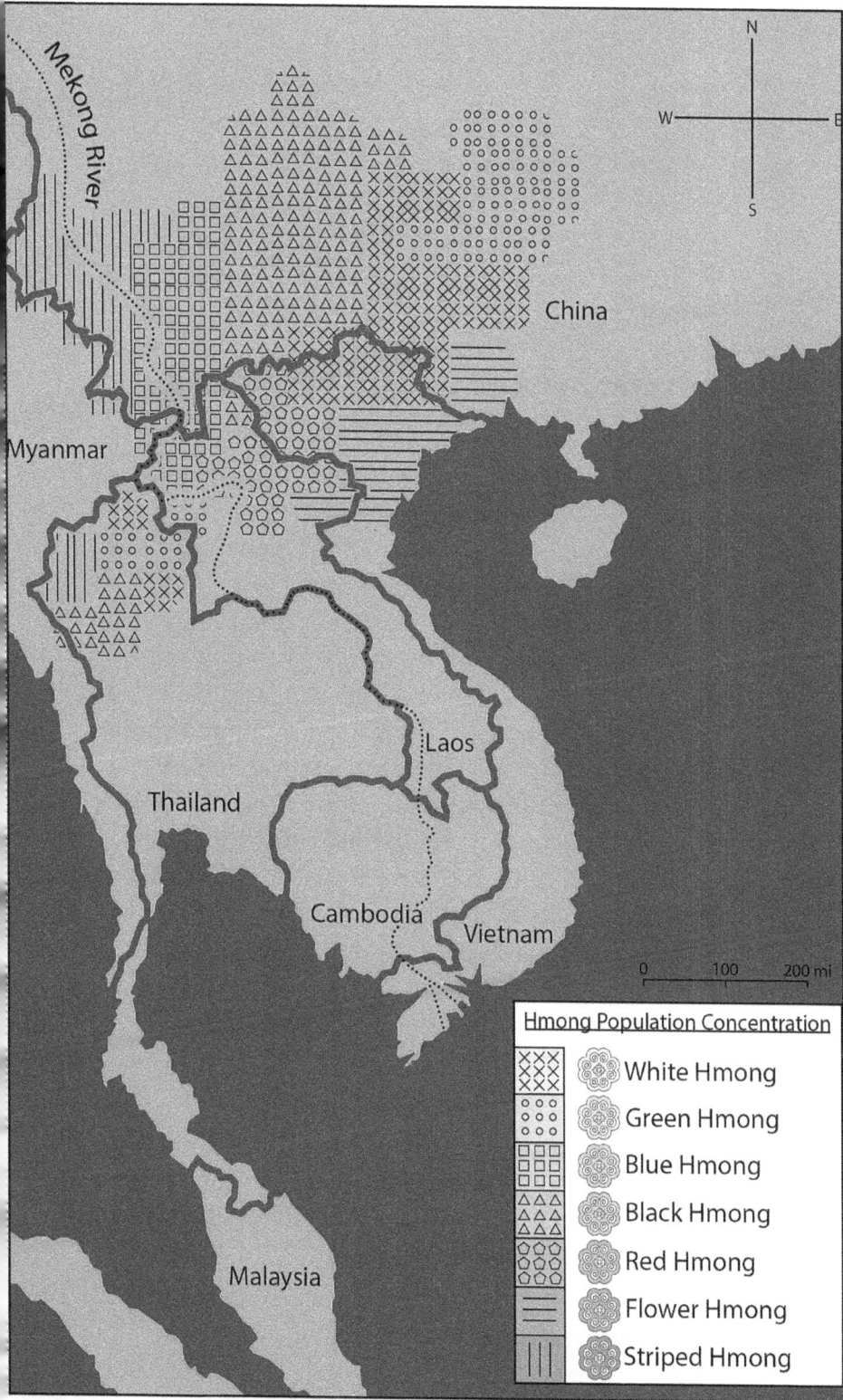

N
W — E
S

Mekong River

China

Myanmar

Laos

Thailand

Cambodia   Vietnam

0   100   200 mi

Malaysia

Hmong Population Concentration

XXX	⚘	White Hmong
○○○	⚘	Green Hmong
□□□	⚘	Blue Hmong
△△△	⚘	Black Hmong
⬠⬠⬠	⚘	Red Hmong
≡≡≡	⚘	Flower Hmong
∣∣∣	⚘	Striped Hmong

Beliefs

56 What are the beliefs of Hmong Americans?

This question has several answers. Some people maintained traditional beliefs in animism. Others became Christian. Some tried Christianity but returned to traditional practices. Others have blended traditional beliefs and practices with Christian ones. Hmong communities support Christian and non-Christian houses of worship. The first American-born Hmong Catholic priest was ordained in St. Paul in 2018. There are also many Hmong American Protestants. The Christian and Missionary Alliance, for example, has its own Hmong District to serve Hmong Americans in their denomination. The Church of Jesus Christ of Latter-day Saints has had as many as 26 congregations with significant Hmong populations, according to the research site Cumorah.com.

57 What are traditional Hmong beliefs?

Traditional Hmong spiritualism embraces animism, ancestor worship and shamans. The shamans intermediate with the spirit world, especially to maintain physical and spiritual connections and health.

58 What is animism?

Animism is a concept and a way to relate to the world, according to the "Open Encyclopedia of Anthropology." People with an "animistic" sensibility attribute sentience— the quality of animation—to a wide universe filled with spirits. Even nonhuman beings, including animals, fish, plants and nonliving objects such as rocks, lakes and technology, are conscious and have intelligence. Animism is applied to survival issues such as health, safety and nutrition. It has been practiced in Africa, South Asia, East Asia, the Arctic and among Indigenous peoples of the Americas. Animism is intensely local. It has no creed, scripture or hierarchy. It does not have the universal God concepts of monotheism and pantheism.

59 What is ancestor worship?

This is the belief that our ancestors remain with us after they pass into the spirit world. Ancestors remain connected to the living and influence the lives and welfare of descendants. For their part, descendants remember their forebears by offering foods and ceremonies. This connection to the spirit world strengthens the family and the Hmong identity.

60 Did the U.S. government want Hmong people to convert?

The U.S. government did not either encourage conversion or support Hmong people's traditional beliefs. However, its policies helped introduce Hmong people to Christianity.

Some policies, such as splitting up families and communities, disrupted traditional practices. Conversion was a byproduct of resettlement. The U.S. wanted to remove its Hmong allies from danger, and Christian churches and resettlement agencies offered help. Wrested from Laos and their traditional rites and practices, some people found Christianity as a way to survive in their new community. Many Hmong see no conflict in combining or blending Christian and traditional religions. Author/researcher Melissa Borja wrote in "Follow the New Way" that Hmong people do not see this as an either/or situation. They see it as natural to blend worlds.

61 Did resettlement churches require conversion?

Most voluntary agencies and churches believed that respectful resettlement would involve helping refugees maintain their beliefs and practices. The mission is to provide help. Certainly, some hosts might hope friendship and curiosity could result in conversion. However, removal from their religious contexts cost some Hmong people their healers, experts and rituals. Some Hmong refugees felt pressure to convert.

62 How many Hmong Americans practice Christianity today?

This is hard to say. One can practice Christianity or traditional religions, both, or have no affiliation at all. Counting churches does not help because while many Hmong communities have physical Christian churches, traditional Hmong religious life does not require a building and has a rich home-centered practice.

63 What are some traditional home-based rituals?

In Hmong culture, many traditions take place among family members. This makes the home an important place of worship and religious practice. It is believed ancestors watch over the house. It is customary to bury the placentas of sons beneath the central pillar and the placentas of girls beneath the homestead bed. Interviews with 94 Hmong people in California detailed the belief that placentas should be buried at home. This was regarded as essential to helping the soul later rejoin ancestors in the spirit world. Many societies respect the role of placentas in ushering in new life. The most sacred part of Hmong houses are the altars of rice paper and gold leaf honoring spirits and bringing prosperity to the family. Different parts of the home such as the central pillar, bedroom, altar, hearth and surrounding area represent the cosmos. Spirits protect and guide from these sections. The lintel above the main door is the txhiaj meej and may be covered with red cloth and silver coins. It protects the family's reputation with anyone who enters. The shrine and items of religious significance are placed in line with the entrance.

64 Is reincarnation a traditional Hmong belief?

The funerary process holds that when a someone dies, their soul goes on a sojourn and must retrace the steps of their life. Ancestors and elders are revered leaders who help guide souls. Traveling to each place the person lived, souls are ready to depart for the afterlife only when they reach the home of their birth. There, they put on their placenta, which the Hmong language calls a jacket, to be reunited with ancestors. In the Hmong afterlife, the soul is reincarnated to be born again as a child.

65 Who are shamans?

The shaman's role is typically one of help and service. The role commands respect but does not convey authority over others. Shamans are healers who are believed to communicate with the spirit world. They are respected for their wisdom and power and can call an ailing person's spirit to return. Shamans can seek intervention from ancestors in health crises. They can appeal for help finding water, for better hunting and for aid resolving challenges to crops. They respond to danger.

66 How does one become a shaman?

The spirit world calls males and females to shamanism. They can be of any age, and they do not choose this themselves. The call is more common for people who have shamans in their families. The transition often begins with a long illness that the person must overcome with the help of spirits. To recover, they must accept this mission. Each community typically has at least one shaman. People can be trained for the position if there is a need.

67 What do shamans do?

Carleton College in Minnesota describes several types of Hmong spiritual healers. They include shamans, herbalists, magical healers and more. Only shamans can perform a diagnostic and healing ceremony called an ua neeb. To help the sick person, the shaman must enter a trance and travel into the spirit world to discover the problem. This requires searching and protection against bad spirits. Helpful tools include split animal horns, finger bells to begin the trance, a gong, a sword and a bench, which represents a horse to ride. The goal is to reunite the person with their soul. Shamans also perform various ceremonies to cure illness. For instance, they perform rituals called hu plig, which means soul-calling. Herbalists cure illness, guided by spirits at a small home altar to create the proper medicine. Hmong magical healers chant using water, metal and incense, according to the "Encyclopedia of Medical Anthropology: Health and Illness in the World's Cultures." They treat burns, broken bones, vomiting, babies' nighttime crying, rashes, children's fright and other illnesses. Healers bring back souls that have been frightened out of the body. They also can mend the soul-body union. They cure with eggs, chickens and rice. They also bless people and secure their health by tying strings around their wrists.

68 What does tying strings signify?

This practice is called khi tes and its main purpose is to keep body and soul united. The practice applies to many situations, in response to sickness and health. It can be for good wishes, to bring joy, luck, for a happy marriage or to protect one from evil or restore spirit and health. White and red strings predominate. Shamans do this, but family and friends do this for each other, too. Less commonly, a string might be tied around an ankle.

69 Do Hmong people believe in good and bad luck?

Some Hmong people hang decorated ornaments, called paj, in doorways, on the rearview mirrors in vehicles or on baby strollers to bring good luck or to ward off evil. Hmong people sometimes also wear forms of jewelry as amulets or charms.

70 How does U.S. culture challenge traditional Hmong spiritual practices?

The greatest challenges for Hmong people in the United States are not direct opposition, but the disruption of communities and families. Borja explains how separation from kin, animistic touchstones and shamans can contribute to a spiritual unmooring. This can hurt people spiritually and physically. Borja notes the difficulty of "adapting a tradition historically rooted in rural settings in Southeast Asia to life in the U.S., a country historically predominated by Christian norms."

71 What is the significance of animal sacrifices?

Animism recognizes animals' souls, and those souls may be used to help unite or lead humans to their souls. Chickens are said to have wings to carry them about in search of souls. Cows and pigs are said to travel on their four legs. The animals may be sacrificed at a market or by a butcher and then taken to a community or family meal.

Ritual and Celebration

72 What are passage rituals?

Rituals mark life from birth until after death. Rituals can vary from household to household and are evolving.

- In the soul-calling ritual hu plig, the shaman performs rites to guide and connect souls to the body in the mortal world.
- Hmong baby welcoming ceremonies involve a hu plig to welcome a spirit world couple who delivers the child's soul when they are physically born.
- Marriage focuses on uniting families and revolves around the groom's family. Traditionally, only one family member a year may be married, and a dowry must be offered to the father of the bride.

73 What are Hmong funeral traditions?

Proper funeral rites help the soul follow its way along the path. Rites include having the body washed and dressing it in special clothes. The deceased were traditionally honored with animal sacrifices and music. These preparations spare the soul from wandering naked and lost in the afterlife.

74 Is there funeral music?

Funeral music laments the loss of loved ones. The qeej is made from six bamboo reeds that are carved and hollowed out. Players blow through a copper mouthpiece to create a light, unique noise. The qeej plays in spoken words, meaning each note is a word of the language. This instrument is used primarily at significant cultural events such as funerals, marriages, and New Year's ceremonies. At funerals, the qeej communicates with the soul of the deceased. Funerals are the only time Hmong people use drums. In some traditions, the drum is made just for the funeral to guide the deceased back to home and ancestors. After the funeral, the drum is destroyed.

75 What are Hmong holiday celebrations?

New Year's is by far the biggest Hmong holiday. Hmong communities hold celebrations with traditional dress, foods and games. This might go on for several days. Individual families, especially if they are not in a large Hmong community, may celebrate at home with soul calling, renewing the household altar and offerings to ancestors. In the Northern Hemisphere, Hmong New Year takes place during the fall harvest from November to December. It follows the lunar calendar, not a specific date. Hmong people also celebrate family events like everyone else such as birthdays. They also observe civic or public holidays of the countries where they live such as Mother's Day, Father's Day, Thanksgiving and Veterans Day.

76 How is the Hmong New Year unique among others?

Traditionally lasting up to 10 days, Hmong New Year is filled with traditional food, music and celebrations. There may be pageants and fine clothes festooned with coins. This is usually before Chinese New Year. Lunar New Year is in early January at the start of the first new moon on the lunar calendar. Each culture has rituals and traditions that make its new year celebrations unique. Hmong people play the ball-tossing game of pov pob. Many Asian countries celebrate the Lunar New Year with their own traditions. Hmong people call the new year "new 30" or "eat 30." This reflects 30 days of good eating. That can mean grilled Hmong sausage, purple sticky rice, papaya salad and more.

Culture

77 What is Hmong embroidery?

"Flower cloths," called paj ntaub, are used to decorate and communicate. Because the Chinese banished the Hmong written language, messages migrated into vivid embroidered patterns. Most themes came from nature. Geometric patterns were common.

One of many popular symbols is the elephant footprint shown here. The elephant is the national animal of Thailand and Laos, formerly the kingdom of Lan Xing (1354-1707). Lan Xing means "Land of a Million Elephants." Laos was thickly forested and sparsely populated, making it a haven for the elephant. In more recent times, deforestation has threatened the elephant's existence. This footprint design was made by April Cha. She is a senior instructional designer at the University of California, San Diego. Her work can be found at aprilmadeshop.etsy.com

78 When is traditional clothing worn now?

New Year's celebrations, weddings and cultural shows are places where Hmong people wear complete traditional outfits or at least some element. They might wear just a purse, tie, belt or shirt with a Hmong design that has been printed or embroidered and indicates their identity. After winning an Olympic gold medal in 2020, U.S. gymnast Sunisa Lee appeared on television with her family. Her mother wore a black jacket with heavy Hmong embroidery.

79 Are there modern Hmong fashions?

The Mount Mary University Magazine in Milwaukee reported that a quarter of its fashion design graduates were of Hmong descent. Many were incorporating traditional colors, fabrics and techniques into clothing.

80 How are art forms changing?

Immersed in western cultures, young Hmong people have taken to all kinds of music, including rap and music videos. Hip-hop is a good fit for its tradition of melding the past and present. Anthropologist Tian Shi has noted that hip-hop gives Hmong artists an outlet to express their identity and share collective memories. Some weave kwv txhiaj poetry into rap lyrics.

81 What is story cloth?

Story cloth is historically important in Hmong culture. In more recent years, Hmong women sew these more elaborate and detailed advancements of flower cloth. Some artists made and sold story cloths to help families earn income. Major themes are Hmong legends or fairy tales, everyday life before the war, the war, and being forced to flee across the dangerous Mekong River. This cloth shows Hmong people attempting to cross the Mekong River from Laos into Thailand and its refugee camps. They approach the broad, rushing river with their belongings on their backs. At upper left is a tree with monkeys in it.

Artist: Sheng Vang of Thailand. Her sister, Yer Vue of Lansing, Michigan, donated the cloth of the Mekong River to the Michigan State Museum Hmong textile collection.

Joseph Yang explained Hmong story cloths at an "Ask a Hmong" event held to inform this guide. View video at: youtu.be/odSE8Pd_Fck or scan the QR code.

82 What are traditional instruments?

There are other traditional instruments besides the qeej and drums. One is the two-string violin. Another is a mouth organ. There are several flute-like instruments. Instrumental music echoes the tonal nature of spoken Hmong.

83 Is there Hmong poetry?

Song poetry, or kwv txhiaj, speaks to the history and resilience of the Hmong people. It is sometimes used in the ball-tossing game. It can also convey mourning or loss. Some say that kwv txhiaj and the qeej echo each other.

84 What are traditional games and recreation?

- Tuj lub, pronounced "too-loo," is a 5,000-year-old outdoor game in which spinning tops are thrown with a line. It has elements similar to bowling and bocce ball.
- Takraw, or kick volleyball, is played over a net that is 7 or 8 feet high. The ball, made of woven rattan or plastic, must be passed and hit with the feet, knees, head or chest. Players leap high in the air and swing upside down to spike the ball with their feet. This competitive team sport is played in several Asian countries.

People also bowl, hunt and fish and play volleyball, soccer and flag football.

85 What is in a traditional Hmong diet?

The Hmong people have lived in many places, and their food reflects that. Hmong people were some of the first people to cultivate rice and this is a major part of their diet. White rice is a staple and eaten at every meal with small portions of meat and vegetables. Throughout their history, Hmong people have raised their own animals and grown their own spices, herbs and vegetables. Hmong dishes incorporate cilantro, chilies, mint, garlic, ginger, spices and other herbs. Fish sauce and oyster sauce are commonly used. Hmong food is most often boiled but can also be stir-fried or steamed. Desserts are not eaten frequently. The traditional Hmong diet is considered to be healthier than American diets.

86 Is Hmong food spicy?

Most Hmong food is not very spicy. However, spice can be added and is often on the side. For example, the hot sauce kua txob, made with chilies, green onions and cilantro, can bring heat to a meal.

87 Is alcohol allowed?

In Hmong culture, drinking is part of celebrations. Social events have drinking customs. People should finish a drink that has been given to them. Joining the toast at a wedding or other event signifies respect. Rice wine has been particularly prevalent. It is made by distilling fermented rice, which the people had grown themselves, so it was an accessible source of alcohol. Rice wine was especially consumed during the New Year celebration, but beer is common today.

88 What is a Hmong knife?

Hmong knives typically have a curved steel blade with a sharp point and a handle made from wood, bone or horn. They have multiple purposes such as farming, hunting small game and defending against wild animals. Knives symbolize strength and courage. They express cultural heritage and identity.

Work and Wealth

89 What occupations do Hmong people pursue?

Some Hmong Americans still farm, but many have found new careers. Researcher Chia Youyee Vang examined census data from 1990-2020. Vang found Hmong people working in manufacturing, education, health care, social assistance and retail. Vang noted "an increase in formal education led many former refugees and second-generation Hmong to work as teachers, nurses and other health-care professionals and within a multitude of social service positions."

90 How much do Hmong workers make?

According to AAPI Data, the median household income for Hmong American households in 2014 was $52,500, about $25 an hour. This was 19th out of the 20 Asian American and Pacific Islander groups in the report. The top three groups were Asian Indians with a median household income of $95,000 a year, Filipinos at $80,000 and Japanese at $78,500. AAPI Data publishes demographic data and policy research.

91 What is the significance of silver jewelry?

The Hmong put their trust in silver and, less frequently, gold. Heavy silver bracelets, earrings, rings, chains, balls and other jewelry can be converted to cash, while paper money can become worthless. Silver is also used to pay dowry. Distinctive pieces of tribal jewelry are worn at New Year's and other holidays. They include heavy neck rings worn by women or babies, and soul lock pendants, called phiaj, resembling padlocks, to keep the body and spirit united.

How U.S. Hmong compare on income

Amounts are annual medians for year-round civilians 16 and older.

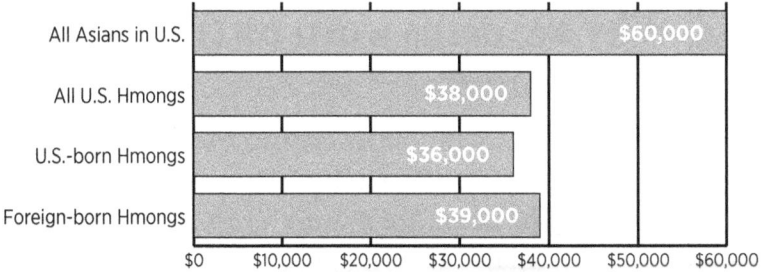

Group	Income
All Asians in U.S.	$60,000
All U.S. Hmongs	$38,000
U.S.-born Hmongs	$36,000
Foreign-born Hmongs	$39,000

Source: Pew Research Center analysis of American Community Survey data, 2019

Graphic by Drew Goretzka

Joseph Yang explained why Hmong people wear coins like those on his vest at an "Ask a Hmong" event held to inform this guide. View the video: youtu.be/E4pN1e6oIUc or scan the QR code.

92 Why are coins worn on traditional Hmong clothing?

The coins have many symbolic meanings. These include indications of family wealth, strength, social status and spiritual health. The coins are mainly worn at traditional celebrations. Originally, Hmong jewelry was made from the high-quality malleable silver in French francs. France has not issued silver coins since 1920, and no francs have been minted since 1999. Today's dresses, shirts and vests bear replicas of the coins.

Health and Medicine

93 How do Hmong health and spirituality intersect?

Health requires a good connection between the body and the spirit. Shamanistic Hmong people believe ancestral spirits or the souls of those who have suffered illness can cause disease, according to the U.S. National Library of Medicine. Some Hmong people believe that sickness comes from separation of the body and soul. Therefore, the remedy must be spiritual. Western medicine does not address that. Therefore, some Hmong Americans may pursue a balance between Western medicine and Hmong spirituality using both systems.

94 What are Hmong health issues?

The Hmong community has greater instances of infectious diseases and cancer. The National Institutes of Health attributes this to limited access to health and nutritional professionals. Rapid changes from active lifestyles and high-fiber diets to less activity and diets high in saturated fats are also concerns.

95 Is there access to appropriate health services?

Cultural, religious and communication differences can impede health care. "The Spirit Catches You and You Fall Down: A Hmong Child, Her American Doctors, and the Collision of Two Cultures" describes deadly consequences of cultural ignorance. In this book, doctors and a young girl's parents continually misunderstand one another. Synapsis: A Health Humanities Journal reported the book became "required reading for many doctors-in-training." The case was cited as an example of a pervasive lack of culturally appropriate health services for the Hmong community.

96 What are some traditional remedies?

Traditional Hmong remedies include herbal medicines or practices aiming to relieve pain or heal broken body parts such as bones. When a Hmong child contracts a common illness, traditional solutions are herbal mixtures that may include chicken, fat or blood. Traditional practices for Hmong people include acupuncture, massage, cupping and coining. Some of these remedies are being studied by Western medicine.

97 What about mental health issues?

According to 2010 research in one Minnesota county, Hmong people are at least twice as likely to have mental health issues such as major depression, general anxiety disorder and post-traumatic stress. These issues may be linked to migration, war trauma, socio-economic problems and multi-generational stressors. Cultural stigma and shame about mental health needs discourage many Hmong people from seeking help. Service gaps can occur in early mental health intervention and in prevention. Furthermore, mental health services are subject to cultural and linguistic misunderstanding.

Politics

98 Do Hmong people vote?

Most Hmong people were ethnic minorities in the places they lived. Some were discouraged by their government, and some were suspicious of it. Organizers are working to increase Hmong American voter turnout. Carolyn Wong, a research associate at the University of Massachusetts, Boston's Institute for Asian American Studies, wrote "Voting Together: Intergenerational Politics and Civic Engagement among Hmong Americans." She explained, "A close examination of the struggles of Hmong Americans to attain participatory freedom and parity can shed light on the process by which new citizens become fully included in national and local communities."

99 Do the major parties recruit Hmong voters?

Close elections and swing-district politics mean major parties are paying more attention. Wisconsin Public Radio reported that Democrats and Republicans courted Hmong American voters in the swing state of Wisconsin in the 2020 campaign. Candidate Joe Biden met with community members and received their endorsement. The state flipped from Republican to Democratic. As president, Biden appointed some Hmong people to positions.

100 Do Hmong people vote as a bloc?

Hmong voters tend to vote for Democrats, but this is not universal. Experience has given them keen interest in refugee issues, and many are close to business or entrepreneurial issues. Both major parties solicit their votes. While Hmong Americans are more likely than many other immigrant groups to be citizens, voter turnout is low.

Hmong People in Politics

More Hmong Americans are exercising their right to vote and to run for office. Several have been elected, especially at the local level and in U.S. districts with large Hmong populations.

Four examples show Hmong political presence growing.

In 2019, Democrats **Samantha Vang**, **Kaohly Her**, **Jay Xiong** and **Tou Xiong** were all elected to the Minnesota House. They joined **Fue Lee**, also a Democrat, who was elected to a second term.

In 2022, a county commission race in Ramsey County, Minnesota, narrowed from seven candidates to two. **Mai Chong Xiong** won with a razor-thin 50.19 percent of the vote, becoming the county's first Hmong American commissioner. The runner-up was **Ying Vang-Pao**, another Hmong American woman.

In 2023, **Sheng Thao** was elected as the first Hmong American mayor of a major U.S. city: Oakland, California.

In 2024, **Mai Xiong**, a Democrat, won election to the Michigan House.

Other Hmong American public officials include:

Foung Hawj: Minnesota state senator (Democratic–Farmer–Labor Party) elected in 2013.

Kazoua Kong-Thao: Board of Education member, St. Paul, Minnesota, 2004-2011.

Choua Lee: In 1991, he became the first elected Hmong American public official in the United States. He served on the St. Paul School Board.

Lormong Lo: First Hmong American appointed to a city council and first to become a city council president in the United States (Republican). It happened in Omaha, Nebraska, in 1994.

Paul C. Lo: In 2013, he became the first Hmong American appointed to serve as a judge in the United States.

Noah Lor: First Hmong American to serve as mayor pro-tem in 2011 in Merced, California.

Steve Ly: First Hmong American mayor, Elk Grove, California, elected in 2016.

Mee Moua: First Hmong American elected to a state house seat. She was elected in Minnesota in 2002. (Democrat)

Mai Vang: Sacramento City Council member (Democrat) elected in 2020.

Tony Vang: First Hmong American elected to the Fresno Unified School Board, elected 2002.

Joe Bee Xiong: Elected to Eau Claire, Wisconsin, City Council in 1996. (Democrat)

May Lor Xiong: First Hmong American to win a Republican U.S. Congressional primary in Minnesota, 2022.

Some other prominent Hmong Americans

Chenue Her: First Hmong male news anchor in the country, joined Iowa WOI-TV in 2021.

Megan Khang: Professional golfer

Sunisa Lee: 2020 U.S. Olympic gold medalist in artistic gymnastics.

Mai Neng Moua: Founder of the Hmong literary magazine Paj Ntaub Voice. Also editor of the first anthology of Hmong American writers, "Bamboo Among the Oaks."

Brenda Song: Actress with Disney, in movies and television, in comedy and dramatic roles.

Fres Thao: Arts advocate, poet, hip-hop artist, multidisciplinary artist and educator.

Bee Vang: Actor and activist, he starred with Clint Eastwood in the 2008 "Gran Torino," the first Hollywood movie to prominently feature Hmong actors.

Chervang Kong Vang: Evangelist, minister and inventor of the Nyiakeng Puachue Hmong writing system used in his United Christians Liberty Evangelical Church.

Gia Vang: Emmy Award-winning journalist, she has anchored at KARE-TV in Minneapolis and at NBC Bay Area News.

Trinity Vang: Storyteller, clothing designer and digital creator. Founder of TRIN Collective featured at Urban Outfitters.

Zoua Vang: Television reporter from 1998 to 2004, she now works in public policy and communications.

Doualy Xaykaothao: Peabody and Edward R. Murrow award-winning freelance and NPR radio and freelance journalist.

Aidan Prince Xiong: Known as BAHBOY, he has been a dancer since the age of 4 and is an actor, singer and vlogger.

Laolee Xiong: A Google engineer, he co-founded the company's official a cappella group, Googapella. As an encore, he jumped to Facebook and set up another a cappella group, the Vocal Network, before moving on.

Tou Ger Xiong: Storyteller, artist and activist, his stories build cultural competency and address racial discrimination.

Fei Yang: 1.6 million people have joined this Michigan State University grad's YouTube channel for her takes on beauty, clothes, shopping, body positivity and relationships.

Xao "Jerry" Yang: 2007 World Series of Poker Main Event champion.

Discussion and Reflection

1. Have you ever wanted to talk with someone but hesitated because you were unsure how to say their name or what to call their group? This is why we made pronunciation one of our first questions. How can people break the ice and the awkwardness when they are meeting someone?

2. There were almost no Hmong people in the United States until 1975. Now, they have one of the highest citizenship rates of any ethnic group. What does this say about their origins and their commitment to citizenship?

3. Some Hmong people blend traditional beliefs with Christianity. Is this unusual, or not? Do other people combine religious practices? Why and how?

4. Animistic and ancestral beliefs and practices are not widespread in the United States. This can pressure people to keep their beliefs quiet or to search for more accepted practices. How might people put in this position feel? What kind of coping mechanisms might they develop?

5. For Hmong people, generations can be compressed and can even overlap. Hmong generations are a blend of birth year, when they or their family came to the United States, and even whether they lived in refugee camps. What kind of gaps or struggles might come along with this?

6. The model minority myth implies that all Asians are successful, yet not all Asian Americans started in the same place. People who are new to the United States and who had different experiences will naturally have some disadvantages. What happens when people judge others as not living up to the stereotypical norm?

7. The model minority myth implies it is easy for Asian Americans to succeed. Does this myth deny people the credit they deserve for individual effort? Does it put unrealistic expectations on some? How?

8. The assimilation vs. adaptation debate is complicated. People want to be accepted as they are, not just for how much they change to accommodate their new culture. What decisions must people make to hold onto their character and be accepted? Has this happened in your family?

9. "Ancestor" comes from Old French and means one who came before. Ancestors and family lineage are important in Hmong culture. How does an ancestral society keep its direction when sudden dislocation cuts its ties to family members and places?

10. What does homeland mean to you? Have you visited it? Do you have family there? What if you did not have a homeland to go back to? Would that affect your sense of identity? Would this make other factors, such as culture or religion, more important?

11. Hmong soldiers were hired, trained and directed by the United States during the CIA's secret war. Many died or were wounded. They are not classified as U.S. veterans because they never served in branches of the U.S. military. Yet some people say Hmong soldiers

and their families should be given veterans' benefits. What are the arguments on both sides?

12. The realities of mountain farming gave Hmong people different conventions for family size, marriage age and even numbers of wives. In the United States, some of those practical conventions are taboo or even against the law. Others might view them with suspicion. How can neighbors better understand ancestral ways?

13. Some women say they have more freedom in the United States than they had under Hmong patrilineal rules. However, new choices can result in pressure to do too many things. What helps people better enjoy new opportunities?

14. Bias Buster guides like this one are intended to answer very basic questions to help people feel more comfortable talking to each other. What are the next steps you can take to learn more about Hmong people?

Resources

Bloomfield, Martha Aladjem. Hmong Americans in Michigan (Discovering the Peoples of Michigan series) East Lansing: Michigan State University Press. 2014.

Borja, Melissa. Follow the New Way: American Refugee Resettlement Policy and Hmong Religious Change. Cambridge: Harvard University Press. 2023.

Cha, Mia, Mai Zong Vue and Steve Carmen. Field Guide to Hmong Culture. Madison: Madison Children's Museum. 2004.

Cha, Ya Po. An Introduction to Hmong Culture. Jefferson: McFarland & Company. 2010.

Dewhurst, C. Kurt and Marsha MacDowell. Michigan Hmong Arts, Textiles in Transition. East Lansing: Michigan State University Museum. 1983.

Fadiman, Anne. The Spirit Catches You and You Fall Down: A Hmong Child, Her American Doctors, and the Collision of Two Cultures. New York City: Farrar, Straus and Giroux (later printing). 2012.

Hamilton-Merritt, Jane. Tragic Mountains: The Hmong, the Americans, and the Secret Wars for Laos, 1942-1992. Bloomington: Indiana University Press. 1999.

Her, V. and M. Buley-Meissner. Hmong and American: From Refugees to Citizens. St. Paul: Minnesota Historical Society Press. 2012.

Hillmer, Paul. A People's History of the Hmong. St. Paul: Minnesota Historical Society Press. 2015.

Laventure, Tom. Shades of Yellow: First Hmong LGBTQ Fundraiser. Twin Cities Daily Planet. Dec. 23, 2009.

Lee, Gary Yia and Nicholas Tapp. Culture and Customs of the Hmong. Denver: Greenwood. 2010.

MacDowell, Marsha. Stories in Thread: Hmong Pictorial Embroidery. East Lansing: Michigan State University Museum. 1989.

Moua, Mai Neng. Bamboo Among the Oaks: Contemporary Writings by Hmong Americans. St. Paul: Minnesota Historical Society Press. 2002.

Quincy, Keith. Hmong: History of a People. Chene: Eastern Washington University Press. 1988.

Rose, Jerry A. and Luce Rose Fischer. The Journalist: Life and Loss in America's Secret War. Tempe: SparkPress. 2020.

Vang, Christopher Thao. Hmong Refugees in the New World: Culture, Community and Opportunities. Jefferson: McFarland & Company, Inc. 2016.

Vang, Chia Youyee. Hmong America: Reconstructing Community in Diaspora. Champaign: University of Illinois Press. 2010.

Vang, Chia Youyee. Hmong in Minnesota (People of Minnesota series). St. Paul: Minnesota Historical Society Press. 2008.

Vang, Mei Der. Afterland: Poems. Minneapolis: Graywolf Press. 2017.

Vang, Mei Der. Yellow Rain. Minneapolis: Graywolf Press. 2021.

Vang, Pa Der. Staring Down the Tiger: Stories of Hmong American Women. St. Paul: Minnesota Historical Society Press. 2020.

Vang, Thomas. A History of the Hmong: From Ancient Times to the Modern Diaspora. Lulu.com. 2013.

Wong, Carolyn. Voting Together: Intergenerational Politics and Civic Engagement among Hmong Americans. Redwood City: Stanford University Press. 2017.

Yang, Kao Kalia. The Latehomecomer: A Hmong Family Memoir. St. Paul: Coffee House Press. 2008.

Yang, Kao-Ly. Planting a Tree. Let's Learn Hmong Language. Kawm Lus Hmoob. Fresno: The Press at California State University. 2021.

Yang, Kou. The Making of Hmong America: Forty Years after the Secret War. Lanham: Rowman & Littlefield. 2017.

Yang, Lue and Judy Lewis. Grandmother's Path, Grandfather's Way: Oral Lore, Generation to Generation. Rancho Cordova: Zellerbach. 1990.

Organizations

Center for Hmong Studies
https://www.csp.edu/center-for-hmong-studies/

The Fresno Center's Hmong Village
https://fresnocenter.org/news/hmong-village/

Hmong American Center
https://www.hmongamericancenter.org/

Hmong American Farmers Association
https://www.hmongfarmers.com/

Hmong American Friendship Association
https://hmongfriendship.org/

Hmong Archives
https://hmongarchives.org/

Hmong Cultural Center
https://www.hmongcc.org/

Hmong Embroidery
https://www.HmongEmbroidery.org

Hmong Institute
https://thehmonginstitute.org/

Hmong Museum
https://hmongmuseummn.org/

Hmong Times online newspaper
https://hmongtimes.com/

Hmong Wisconsin Chamber of Commerce
https://hmongchamber.org/

Website of Hmong anthropologist Gary Yia Lee
https://www.garyyialee.com/

Video resources

Between Two Worlds: The Hmong Shaman in America. Collective Eye Collection. 1984.

Gran Torino. Eastwood, Clint; Michael Stevens, Kyle Eastwood, Lennie Niehaus. Germany/USA/Australia, 2008.

Growing up Hmong at the Crossroads: Unbecoming a Refugee. Directed, written and produced by Safoi Babana-Hampton. East Lansing: Michigan State University, 2017.

Hmong Memory at the Crossroads. Directors, Safoi Babana-Hampton, Swarnavel Eswaran Pillai, Cyril Payen. East Lansing: Michigan State University, 2015.

Hmong Pioneers: Honoring the First Wave. 2016. SPNN Documentary. 2016.

The Hmong and the Secret War: The Hmong American Story. Valley PBS. 2017.

Minnesota Remembers Vietnam: America's Secret War. Twin Cities Public Television. 2017.

Our Story

The 100 Questions and Answers series springs from the idea that good journalism should increase cross-cultural competence and understanding. Most of our guides are created by Michigan State University journalism students.

We use journalistic interviews to surface the simple, everyday questions that people have about each other but might be afraid to ask. We use research and reporting to get the answers and then put them where people can find them, read them and learn about each other.

These cultural competence guides are meant to be conversation starters. We want people to use these guides to get some baseline understanding and to feel comfortable asking more questions. We put a resources section in every guide we make and we arrange community conversations. While the guides can answer questions in private, they are meant to spark discussions.

Making these has taught us that people are not that different from each other. People share more similarities than differences. We all want the same things for ourselves and for our families. We want to be accepted, respected and understood.

Please email your thoughts and suggestions to series editor Joe Grimm at joe.grimm@gmail.com, at the Michigan State University School of Journalism.

Related Books

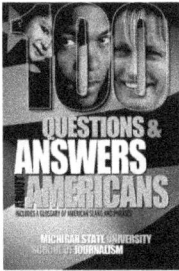

100 Questions and Answers About Americans
Michigan State University School of Journalism, 2013

This guide answers some of the first questions asked by newcomers to the United States. Questions represent dozens of nationalities coming from Africa, Asia, Australia, Europe and North and South America. Good for international students, guests and new immigrants.

ISBN: 978-1-939880-20-8

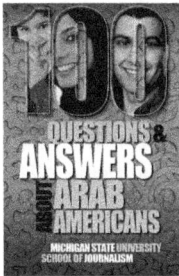

100 Questions and Answers About Arab Americans
Michigan State University School of Journalism, 2014

The terror attacks of Sept. 11, 2001, propelled these Americans into a difficult position where they are victimized twice. The guide addresses stereotypes, bias and misinformation. Key subjects are origins, religion, language and customs. A map shows places of national origin.

ISBN: 978-1-939880-56-7

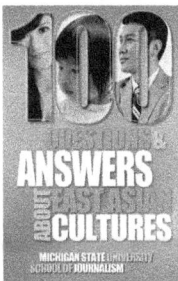

100 Questions and Answers About East Asian Cultures
Michigan State University School of Journalism, 2014

Large university enrollments from Asia prompted this guide as an aid for understanding cultural differences. The focus is on people from China, Japan, Korea and Taiwan and includes Mongolia, Hong Kong and Macau. The guide includes history, language, values, religion, foods and more.

ISBN: 978-939880-50-5

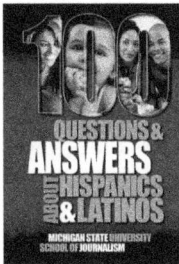

100 Questions and Answers About Hispanics & Latinos
Michigan State University School of Journalism, 2014

This group became the largest ethnic minority in the United States in 2014 and this guide answers many of the basic questions about it. Questions were suggested by Hispanics and Latinos. Includes maps and charts on origin and size of various Hispanic populations.

ISBN: 978-1-939880-44-4

Print and ebooks available on Amazon.com and other retailers.

Related Books

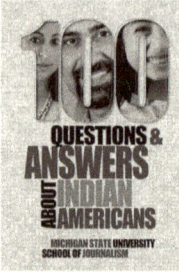

100 Questions and Answers About Indian Americans
Michigan State University School of Journalism, 2013

In answering questions about Indian Americans, this guide also addresses Pakistanis, Bangladeshis and others from South Asia. The guide covers religion, issues of history, colonization and national partitioning, offshoring and immigration, income, education, language and family.

ISBN: 978-1-939880-00-0 m

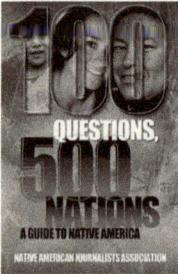

100 Questions, 500 Nations: A Guide to Native America
Michigan State University School of Journalism, 2014

This guide was created in partnership with the Native American Journalists Association. The guide covers tribal sovereignty, treaties and gaming, in addition to answers about population, religion, U.S. policies and politics. The guide includes the list of federally recognized tribes.

ISBN: 978-1-939880-38-3

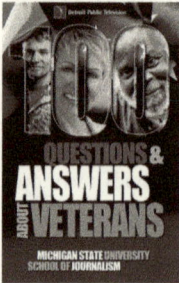

100 Questions and Answers About Veterans
Michigan State University School of Journalism, 2015

This guide treats the more than 20 million U.S. military veterans as a cultural group with distinctive training, experiences and jargon. Graphics depict attitudes, adjustment challenges, rank, income and demographics. Includes six video interviews by Detroit Public Television.

ISBN: 978-1-942011-00-2

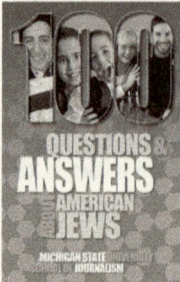

100 Questions and Answers About American Jews
Michigan State University School of Journalism, 2016

We begin by asking and answering what it means to be Jewish in America. The answers to these wide-ranging, base-level questions will ground most people and set them up for meaningful conversations with Jewish acquaintances.

ISBN: 978-1-942011-22-4

Related Books

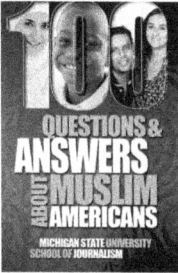

100 Questions and Answers About Muslim Americans
Michigan State University School of Journalism, 2014

This guide was done at a time of rising intolerance in the United States toward Muslims. The guide describes the presence of this religious group around the world and inside the United States. It includes audio on how to pronounce some basic Muslim words.

ISBN: 978-1-939880-79-6

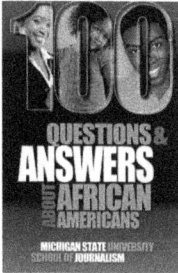

100 Questions and Answers About African Americans
Michigan State University School of Journalism, 2016

Learn about the racial issues that W.E.B. DuBois said in 1900 would be the big challenge for the 20th century. This guide explores Black and African American identity, history, language, contributions and more. Learn more about current issues in American cities and campuses.

ISBN: 978-1-942011-19-4

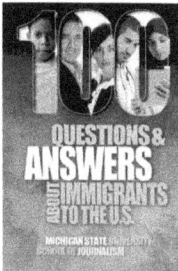

100 Questions and Answers About Immigrants to the U.S.
Michigan State University School of Journalism, 2016

This simple, introductory guide answers 100 of the basic questions people ask about U.S. immigrants and immigration in everyday conversation. It has answers about identity, language, religion, culture, customs, social norms, economics, politics, education, work, families and food.

ISBN: 978-1-934879-63-4

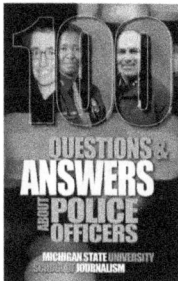

100 Questions and Answers about Police Officers
Michigan State University School of Journalism, 2018

This simple, introductory guide answers 100 of the basic questions people ask about police officers, sheriff's deputies, public safety officers and tribal police. It focuses on policing at the local level, where procedures vary from coast to coast. The guide includes a resource about traffic stops.

ISBN: 978-1-64180-013-6

Print and ebooks available on Amazon.com and other retailers.

Related Books

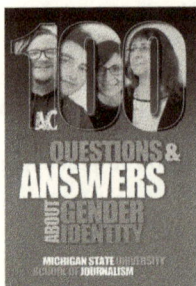

100 Questions and Answers About Gender Identity
Michigan State University School of Journalism, 2017

The guide is written for anyone who wants quick answers to basic, introductory questions about transgender people. It is a starting point people who want to get a fast grounding in the facts.

ISBN: 978-1-641800-02-0

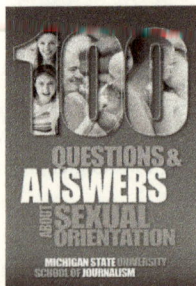

100 Questions and Answers About Sexual Orientation
Michigan State University School of Journalism, 2018

This clear, introductory guide answers 100 of the basic questions people ask about people who are lesbian, gay, bisexual or who have other sexual orientations. The questions come from interviews with people who say these are issues they frequently get asked about or wish people knew more about.

ISBN: 978-1-641800-27-3

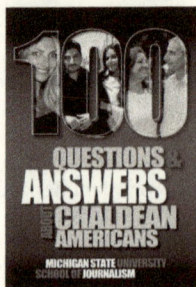

100 Questions and Answers About Chaldean Americans
Michigan State University School of Journalism, 2019

This guide has sections on identity, language, religion, culture, customs, social norms, economics, politics, education, work, families and food. It is written for those who want authoritative answers to basic, questions about this immigrant group from Iraq.

ISBN: 978-1-934879-63-4

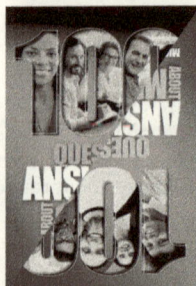

100 Questions and Answers About Gen X Plus
100 Questions and Answers About Millennials
Michigan State University School of Journalism, 2019

This is a double guide in the Bias Busters series. It is written for those who want authoritative answers about these important generations and how we all work together.

ISBN: 978-1-641800-47-1

Related Books

True Border: 100 Questions and Answers About the
U.S.-Mexico Frontera
Borderzine: Reporting Across Fronteras, 2020

This guide was developed by the University of Texas/ Borderzine for the Bias Busters cultural competence series. The guide is written for people who want authoritative answers about the U.S.-Mexico border region and get up to speed quickly on this important topic.

ISBN: 978-1-641800-60-0

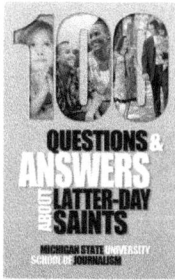

100 Questions and Answers About Latter-day Saints
Michigan State University School of Journalism, 2020

This guide is written for those who want authoritative answers to basic questions about the Latter-day Saints faith. It relies extensively on the Church of Jesus Christ of Latter-day Saints writings and suggests resources for greater depth.

ISBN: 978-1-641800-90-7

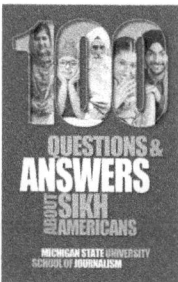

100 Questions and Answers About Sikh Americans
Michigan State University School of Journalism, 2022

Sikhism is the fifth largest religion in the world. It is a young religion, having been founded in 1469. It has been in the United States for almost 150 years, but is still relatively unknown. The questions in this guide were created by interviewing Sikhs.

ISBN: 978-1-641801-43-0

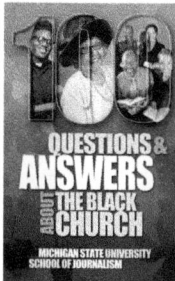

100 Questions and Answers About The Black Church
Michigan State University School of Journalism, 2022

Forged in the furnace of U.S. segregation, the Black Church is the pillar of African American communities across the country. This guide answers the call that TIME magazine raised in a headline, "To understand America, you need to understand the Black Church."

ISBN: 978-1-641801-55-3

Print and ebooks available on Amazon.com and other retailers.

Related Books

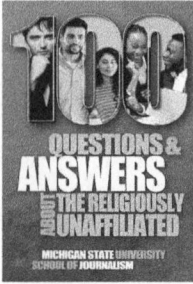

100 Questions and Answers About the Religiously Unaffiliated
Michigan State University School of Journalism, 2024

Sometimes generally referred to as "the nones," agnostics, atheists, humanists, freethinkers, secularists and skeptics compose one of the fastest growing faith categories in the United States. Some people face discrimination as nonbelievers, despite their varied and strong beliefs, values and morals.

ISBN: 978-1-641-801-66-9

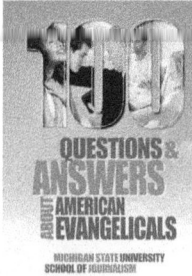

100 Questions and Answers About American Evangelicals
Michigan State University School of Journalism, 2024

Evangelical Christianity is one of the largest religions in the United States and wields tremendous political power. Learn about the core beliefs that tie this varied, decentralized group together. See how it became a political powerhouse and where it gets its political lean.

ISBN: 978-1-64180-195-9

www.ingramcontent.com/pod-product-compliance
Lightning Source LLC
Chambersburg PA
CBHW022036090426
42741CB00007B/1086